Begin Empty-Handed

Also by Gail Martin

———

The Hourglass Heart, 2003

BEGIN EMPTY-HANDED

Gail Martin

PERUGIA PRESS
FLORENCE, MASSACHUSETTS
2013

Perugia Press extends deeply felt thanks to the many individuals whose generosity made the publication of *Begin Empty-Handed* possible. Perugia Press is a tax-exempt, nonprofit 501(c)(3) corporation publishing first and second books of poetry by women. To make a tax-deductible donation, please contact us directly or visit our Web site.

Book design by Susan Kan, Jeff Potter, and Gail Martin.
Author photograph by Kaitlin LaMoine Martin.
Cover photograph is "Still Life with Woodpecker and Scissors," by Kimberly Witham, used with permission of the artist (www.kimberlywitham.com).

Library of Congress Cataloging-in-Publication Data
Martin, Gail
  [Poems. Selections]
  Begin Empty-Handed / Gail Martin.
      pages   cm
  Poems.
  ISBN 978-0-9794582-6-2 (alk. paper)
  I. Title.
  PS3613.A7785B44 2013
  811'.6--dc23
                        2013013886

Perugia Press
P.O. Box 60364
Florence, MA 01062
info@perugiapress.com
http://www.perugiapress.com

To my parents for what they taught me and continue to teach me

To George, my heart and true companion

CONTENTS

Three

BEGIN EMPTY-HANDED

ONE

JUGGLER

That man alone on the spot-lit stage juggling knives of different heft and blade length: cleaver, butcher knife, stiletto. It seems dangerous, but he scoffs, like a dog wanting more than walks and water, bored with the predictability of what comes next. He asks the audience to pitch in. Purses open in the dark and suddenly nail clippers, lipstick, a warm wallet full of children's faces. From stage left come eye glasses, a corkscrew, a folded handkerchief. From the right, a condom and a blue glass paperweight that looks like the world. A wedding ring. He accepts each of them, tosses them up into the expanding circle, five items, nine, twelve. He could juggle a horse if you threw it at him. Suddenly, a small caliber handgun, Smith & Wesson. He doesn't hesitate, doesn't check to see if the safety is on or off. He just continues to pay attention, catch whatever gets thrown at him and put it in motion, the relief of releasing it for a moment each time it circles, and then gravity, that loyal dog, bringing it back.

Begin Empty-Handed

My liturgy is easy: morning's first bird,
warm rain, the peepers' glee. The east sky

lighting up. But still, there will be a fork
in my day, some junction of blessing

and question. Call the hawk wheeling
over the plowed field abundance,

casting a shadow as he flies. This
is not a simple economy, where loss

is the only bird at the feeder. Consider
one world—white tulips in a crystal jar,

Japanese pearl divers, skirts flaring
in the light then becoming the light.

A girl who confesses the reason she loves
elephants is because they mourn their dead.

We used to have a minister who moved
his hands to contain or punctuate.

On the one hand ... and on the other ...
this scaffolding a formula to say almost

nothing. Yesterday, I found deer bones, gore
gone but some fur clutched to a joint

that looked gnawed off. It takes me a while,
studying its size, the limits of its hingey nature

to determine *knee*. And suddenly I miss
my brother who understands all these things,

as well as the helplessness of it, the torn
full skirt of it, the spilled cold milk of it.

The sky wears black serge pants while
hemming up another pair for tomorrow
night. A bit shorter, but you won't notice.
Some nights the blue pill brings a dream
where a young girl is trying not to cry
in the sheep pasture, stuck where her brothers
eyed the watery gap and mossy stones and sailed
to the other side. We didn't know about *E. coli*
then, how our waders must have buzzed with it.
By the time I was ten, I'd pared my list of things
I was scared of down to four: the high board,
hoods and kidnappers, blue racers, and shaking
hands with Uncle John who'd lost four fingers
in the cornpicker. I pushed the scared parts of me
away, like the two finches my mother watched
nudge a dead fledgling off the edge of her deck.

THE THERAPIST WATCHES BIRDS

The birds are manic, wild. They are the best
part of December. Their questions
are what interest me, slashing and punctuating
the air with their abrupt arrivals
and leave-takings, their mild plagiarisms.

               Why, yesterday, then,
same seed, time of day, weather, were there
none at the feeder?

Today the nuthatches are in freefall,
everything pitched to survival. And while
this is also true for some people, mostly now,
I do not see them in my office. And mostly
that is a relief.

             What I do is dream about them.
The man who cut his hard cherry trees to pay
his hospital bills—a man whose father, drunk,
had lined them up in pajamas for Russian roulette,
whose mother hung him up on a hook in the barn
for two days to calm down. He'd planted his trees
so close, he had to cut down three before any
had room to fall.

I don't worry about these birds. I can't fail
them, plenty of berries just feet from the window,

presumably bugs. These bright planes would take off
and land without me tromping out food.

                    With people, each pause
in conversation is room for a hundred
different responses.

I say all paths lead to the same place
but I don't believe it. Some lead through groves
of cherry trees and some to water, some
to the cliff hanging over it all.

It's not always about shoring up dams and levees.
This morning, she arrived nearly hypothermic
and said she'd been standing in the lake up to her neck
for a while to keep from hurting herself. I had to tell her
standing in ice water in winter is hurting yourself.
She believes that maybe it doesn't count because
it doesn't leave marks. I understand this and I don't.

I don't care deeply about birds. I enjoy them.
They raise questions in a casual way. I have found
them with their necks broken at the base
of my window. There are cats and fox and snakes.
Some nights are just too cold. I am not responsible.

                 Right now, as I watch,

a chickadee is pedaling in space, outwaiting
a wren at the feeder. He looks like someone running
off a cliff in a cartoon, suddenly realizing
the ground beneath him has fallen away.

First Session

You come to keen for your daughter, dead
by oncology just two weeks. In my notes,

I write down *burnt caramel frosting, chocolate
cupcakes made with stout.* You tell me how

her head swelled up from the steroids, describe
spasms and hemorrhage. I write *dad riding*

*in the trunk of a Chevy Coupe from Michigan
to Missouri, 1940.* I'm on the dock, arguing

about minnows. I say *pedal,* he says he couldn't
think of a worse verb to describe the way they

move. I say *flicker* then and *skitter,* but the water
is so clear and minnow rhymes with winnowing,

that gradual scattering and blowing away. Which
is what's happening to my parents who walk

holding hands, back to shore.

                     Your words disappear
faster than watches from the wrists of old people

in nursing homes. You sleep on a blow-up mattress

in the living room, her ashes on the bed beside you.

You want to know if that is sick. I write down
the summer I underlined much of Corinthians,

and *what boy doesn't love a shipwreck?*

THE LONGER YOU RUB YOUR HANDS, THE CLEANER THEY BECOME

I would rather be talking about why the bees are disappearing
or whether that star—right there—is the new one, brighter

than the rest. We might discuss how much it would hurt
if a hummingbird hit the side of your head at top speed,

or whether sheets from Egyptian cotton smell like camels.
A woman stands in front of a blind white horse. That is one memory.

A black butterfly with a wingspan wide as my hand.
But that chicken. The way shreds of raw breast kept sticking

to my fingers, the struggle with those roly tendons. I remember
I wanted a nail brush, a bath, lather. I remember the cutting board

I couldn't scrub enough, three dull knives I avoided all the next day.
I'm trying to pray this off me, this particular quiet, a room

where someone has stopped the radio. Grief, a seed, has planted
itself between us. Some tear-shaped bird is screeching for its mother.

HIKING THE RIVER WITH HANNAH

I'm having trouble walking uneven ground;
my foot's Motrin'd and taped, tendon inflamed.
The best I can do is move the pain around.

Hannah's arm, a lattice of slashes astounds
me. At her wrist, the tattoo: *LIVE*. No one's to blame
for my trouble walking this uneven ground—

nature's indifferent, roots trip and confound
all of us, though there's grace in this terrain.
All we can do is move the pain around

when suffering starts with a young mother drowned,
moves to an ankle, heart. Not much to sustain
my limping. Walking this uneven ground

I'm angry. How can I find peace surrounded
by a landscape of trouble dawning plain
daily? It's all I can do to shift it around.

Hannah's worn out, unsure where she's bound.
I turn toward home, my farewell hollow, lame.
I'm having trouble walking holy ground,
I'm barely able to move the pain around.

ANGER, NO ORPHAN

Shhhhhh … anger's napping, sucking her thumb, full of it.
Keep anger warm and kiss her hot head; rock this red baby,
her wrinkly face, her no eyebrows. You will need to tell her
again and again that you love her more than her snappy
cousin sarcasm, that you will help her grow bigger if that is
what she needs to do. You can feed her tapioca with a small
spoon, rub oil into her hands and heels, but you don't have
to. She's a perfect knot of knowing, curled in your arms. Her
purses of eggs are delicate, unzipped. She will teethe on the
white stone from Lake Superior. When she rakes blue plates
off the table, you will hate her and begin to pretend she does
not belong to you.

THE HEART IN THE CAR WASH

When I found it, I couldn't tell if it was animal
or human, shining there in the cold corner

on the wet floor, not pulsing, not steaming, no
electrical charge. Larger than two fists, a wet mop

head, a ham. Not an overweight plum or bunch
of grapes left too long, halo of fruit flies hovering.

I am telling you what it looked like, what it made
me think: cows, *bovine*. A bull's spleen, a bull frog

crouching. That kind of weight. Or a kind of bomb,
the way childbirth is a bomb, the purple wetness, why

you'd never wear your own nightgown, why you'd rip
a nightgown off. It looked like Jesus' heart, purpled

and taxed. I can see it stuck on top of my Christmas
tree. I can see it as a pair of wet socks swollen and balled.

Last winter I couldn't touch my car without throwing off
sparks. I grew afraid to reach for the door handle, to adjust

my mirror. I wore rubber boots and gloves, tried to be sure
I was grounded. The day I found the heart I met a man

who told me he'd experienced the same thing. He felt
the same fear, the same shame. I was the first one he told.

I Don't Want to Say How Lost I've Been

Missed my road by Cathead Point, took the wrong loop on the trail at Port Oneida. Got so turned around on Voice Road by North Bar Lake I couldn't speak for three days. I went to the IGA after it closed. Good Harbor Grill doesn't serve dinner. I never know which side of the road the river will be on. It takes me a while to realize I'm lost. You could call that confidence or part of the problem. Lake = north, lake = north, I say to myself, but lake = west and northwest a bit down the road, and there's a lake to the east here too. A friend's husband draws a map by hand each time she leaves, CANADA at the top, MEXICO at the bottom. The oceans are implied. This is to help her know if she overshoots a turn. I understand. I love maps, the names, the blue shapes of lakes and rivers. I can find my way anywhere theoretically. What's hard is the YOU ARE HERE part. And it isn't exactly loneliness, although I'm calling it that.

When You Spot a Man Drowning

Go after him only as a last resort. First throw boat cushions, mildewed life rings, the bumpers and buoys you use to keep your boat from rocking against the dock. Before you find yourself in deep water, toss a hunk of driftwood into his path, a paddle. Try a thermos with its vacuum-packed air, a rope tied to your dog, a milk jug. Try the anchor if nothing else floats. If you go after him, memorize the shore, line up the house you've known all your life with the hemlock's tall shadow. Forget what you know about the cross-chest carry, surface approaches, block and parry. Keep the victim submerged and at arm's length while you check if the flailing indicates waving or drowning. Ask yourself if he really wants to survive. He's weighed down, filled his pockets with dog hair, sand, Cheerios, quarters, not air. A peculiar bitterness he hoards. Ask where the tiny bubbles of happiness lodge, that last exhalation of joy.

WHEN I SEE THE CARVED COCONUT LEFT BY PUTU MUDA, I KNOW

I could not live in Bali, where
    the highest purpose is to please
the gods, where women leave tiny boats
    of banana leaf heaped with blossom,
perhaps a slice of areca nut, a woven palm, a stick
    of jasmine incense piled on dashboards, thresholds,
office desks.   Petals are placed to return
    to earth at crossroads where troubled
spirits congregate. People walk on them. Dogs nose in, a chicken
    pecks up the offerings. They wither in the sun, wash away
in rain. I would be gathering them up.
    I can't even leave the lilies here in the cabin for someone
new, can't spread my leftovers on the earth for birds.
    Not even this cold white rice, a particularly fragrant basmati.
My dog, waiting for me at home, loves it so.

CRAWL

I sat beside an off-duty pilot once.
He told me to keep a cup of water on my tray.

In case of fire, soak my napkin in it and press it
over my nose and mouth. The floor lights

will not be working, the crew will be panicked
or dead. *Crawl*, he said, *count seats to the exit.*

There have been times I thought I wouldn't make
a clean getaway. I remember the crash near Detroit

seeded I-94 with wreckage. Among the shoes,
seat cushions, and reading glasses, the alcoholic's

primer. I picture the Big Book open on his lap,
him counting twelve steps.

Before She Was
Afraid of Water

She trawls for something without a
name. Rain salts the glassy surface,
sounds like pea gravel she throws
toward her brother's window when
her parents lock her out. Sometimes
it works. Sometimes he is too drunk
to wake up. Once her father. She
knows he watches her in the driveway,
making some boy into what she needs.
Some faces only a daughter can see.
Rough angels now, and when she
wakes up with bruises, she knows the
dead have been touching her again.
She sees herself as Santa Barbara, how
it all used to be under the ocean. She
keeps finding shells in the hills.

THE ESCAPE GOAT

Two goats were chosen on the Day of Atonement. The first was sacrificed
while the escapegoat was taken into the wilderness and released.
—Leviticus 16

Not a Tennessee fainting goat, humming with worry, keeling
over stiff-legged, paralyzed by panic. But no mountain
goat either, toes like pliers on rock, sure-footed and climbing

since birth. Not lusty nor brave nor balanced, no nimble contortionist
for love, always landing on her feet. *I'm tired of being their escape*
goat, she cries. This goat is the worse for wear, frankly crabby, her heart

tired as linen. Hand-stitched saddlebags slap her flanks, swollen
with corn cobs and legacies, shadows cast by the family tree. She never
conceived a landscape like this. Some days it's hard to know if she's the goat

to be released or the one turned on the spit for the wrongdoings of others.
A daughter suggests there's not much difference, implies life
in the wilderness would be brief, what with bobcats and wolves.

Each possibility presses down on her and she begins to chew, swallowing
all of it: hay to sin, razor blades to crackers, every
Bible verse that fails to mention grace.

TWO TRUTHS AND A LIE

My father was a surgeon and my mother was a sandhill crane. Or my mother delivered babies and my father was a starfish. There were two of them. My father fed my mother peanut butter and raisin bran every morning. Friday nights we'd play two truths and a lie over and over and I learned love's habits. Grown men held golf umbrellas over us, sensible harbors from raindrops or bee swarm, fed me peppermints warm from their pockets. Sometimes it would storm paper and the trees would flatten and turn white. Two nights ago, the bark peeled from our last living birch tree. One of us has a scar on the throat that still itches. It may be a paper cut. The family engine never sputters, though my brother has never been happy. All his yachts are leakers. My own diamond shoes are too tight, and then there is my closed heart. The rattlesnake curled on the threshold? We toss him on the woodpile near the cedars to keep down mice, their rustle and scurry on the heap. Mother dreamed she heard them playing thimbles in the eaves. Even now, I monitor the calcium and gold levels in her blood, its sweet smell and gush. And this year, for the first time, I howl as the white flowers go into the dirt, their frowsy skirts spilling over the clay pot's lip. The landscape is cramped here, no mountains stretch their faces to cloud, no water spills its trout off the world's edge. House house house house. Tree tree tree, you can't see much at all.

Ordinary House I

No one enters or leaves
without slamming the door.
Some nights, following dinner,
this room smells just like spent shells.

AUGENBLICK

Here in the country, it's so quiet you can hear
eggs boiling two farms over, shells clicking against
each other in rolling water that tastes like iron.
It would be easy to set myself on fire tonight,
a hundred votives on the table, red silk stole, wine.

Before I came here, one daughter sent e-mail
headed "Snowing in Brooklyn." Another circles a boy
who may not love her enough. The youngest considers
getting a small tattoo, a German word on the back
of her knee, *Augenblick*, meaning moment.

In this cabin, my phone doesn't work. I sleep
with heated rice sacks instead of my husband. When
we lived in France we warmed our sheets with bricks
but no one told us to wrap them first in flannel.
I ended up in a cold bed with a square burned

down through it. Tonight, sacks heat my face,
my feet, cradle my neck. I can move one between
my knees or breasts, pull it close in my arms like a child, like
the babies I nursed without falling asleep. Tonight
I will dream of sewing machines whose needles snap

striking rice kernels as they stitch up the seams.
Or of someone stealing my silver rings. Of school.
How our dreams love the classroom, desks lined up

in rows designed to expose us in our failures. It's
sometimes hard to know where you've gone wrong.

Tomorrow the snow will keep falling and though I
don't know it yet, I'll find my sheets shredded, mattress
chewed by mice. I'll hike white fields, come across a tomato, far
from the garden. Heavy as a croquet ball, without a blemish
on it. For a moment, I'll take its weight in my hand.

WHEN PIPPI LONGSTOCKING WAS MY MOTHER

We sailed the seven seas and had it good. The world
was a wild and better place. We answered to no one.
Back then, the building tops sprouted domes like fat turnips
in purple and green. Trees grew from windows, no two
alike, no straight lines messed up our balconies, our towers.
Grandma was an angel up in heaven who peeked down
at us, her husband a cannibal king. One day mother would dance
with the burglars who'd come to rob our house, the next day, play
tag with police. It was all the same to her; she always came out on top.
My mother loved a monkey named Mr. Nillson, drank coffee
and had two friends. She was the strongest person in the world.
She could lift horses if she wanted to and, oh boy, she wanted to.
She never abandoned me. When I left her, she handed me
her beat-up suitcase, bursting with golden coins.

He Explains

One syringe load of Sodium
Pentothal, fast-acting barbiturate
for rapid, pleasant induction of
anesthesia. We found a vein in her
ear and made a good vena puncture.
She went to sleep immediately
and then we opened the abdomen.
Dogs have individual pouches or
uteri where each new puppy is
sequestered. We took them out
without opening the sacks. They
never breathed. Closed the belly
in layered sutures as I feared she
would dig at any she could get at.
Brought her home the next day.
That's the story; don't tell your
sensitive daughter as she will think
I am an animal killer or something.
Seemed like the thing to do at the
time with your mother so pregnant.
Don't get me in trouble, the statute
of limitations might begin with
discovery, which is now.

If Marriage Is an Aquarium

Monterey Bay Aquarium, Easter

My husband and I watch a male sea horse
squeeze out replicas of self, pale as a fingernail

or communion wafer. *I hope you two will be as happy
as we thought we would be* reads the wedding card

we make up. These jellies bloom and drift
through three stories of blue light. Some are pink

like the girl's bedroom we painted together once.
She grew up to resent gender. A machine spins

to create current, to keep them from being trapped
in the corners. Nothing here knows that it's Easter.

The schools of sardines silver past, finger-sized, then
flash in a new direction. Fast as a slap, they respond

to their own watery code. The child behind us whines
for whales. Whales are the opposite of sardines,

blood vessels big enough for me to swim through.
I can't explain why sardines are my favorite.

BINOCULAR

It is your binoculars I want when you die.
The way you wanted your father's cherry

wood humidor. The way Bruce wanted his
father's black figure skates and in lacing them

on, received a vision of his father, young,
unfurling across the ice, arms floating up.

I want to see you at dusk at the lake, arm
casual on the window of the station wagon, tour

guide of the dump, searching out deer and bear.
I was never quick enough to spot them or maybe

they were never there. I couldn't focus the lenses
or position them against my glasses.

I was the only one in the back seat paying attention.
Me, madras shorts and pixie cut, trying to see

what you saw, what you said was there.

UNCOUPLING

For forty years, my dad picked up mittens
dropped from chairlifts. People took one off

to wipe their nose, apply Chapstick, and
gone. He has a drawer full of singles, more

rights than lefts, leather and insulated.
I remember the night I lay beside my husband

and thought, all right then. Now we are together
for eternity. I said that word, *eternity*, not knowing

what it means, relating it in some vague way
to galaxies or Roman sandals with bronze disks

hammered into their leather. Though perhaps
that is *antiquity*. How many ways we decide

to come together and separate. My mother says
she wants to die before my father. Some days

she practices lifting out the bolt on the clasp
that holds her boxcar to the train, knuckle couplers

yearning to let go. I have felt it just once, driving
toward trouble, the pull of an old maple

next to the road, beckoning arms familiar, ready
to catch me, right where the route curves north.

Two

LETTERS TO AN INVENTED SISTER

i.

There are too many heartbeats
in this house at times, a drowned moth
in the blind dog's water bowl.
When I confuse the woodpecker
with my own pulse, I think about
the tender way morning unbuttons
the day, the deer with their antler
buds and scars who surround me
like circling wagons. And when mist
lifts off the lake, there's nothing else.
Some water birds, their wings.

ii.

Today I left the water for a few hours,
the fields consoled me with Angus calves,
small black boxcars, their square heads
above the grass. I keep thinking about Anna,
her violated heart. I have long held the theory
that one sets drooping tulips in ice water
to stiffen their spines. I read about a man
collapsed and weeping on the basement stairs
while his wife stirred pancakes in the kitchen
five steps away. Neither able to help the other.
Helplessness is not, however, impotence,
and I'm off to buy whitefish.

iii.

Do you remember the last winter in Sanibel?
Florida so cold, the iguanas dropped out
of the trees. And Mother throwing a party
with that little camp stove on which she refused
to cook meat. She spent hours peeling skin
off her legs and feeding the gulls, always
endorsing the luck of an open wound. Father
bought clementines, I remember, those small,
unmessy oranges from Spain. We admired
their compactness, their unseeded juice.
He told me that night he could no longer lift
the watering can, said it was *disconcerting*,
almost a feeling word. What he didn't say
was how grief had jumped and rolled him,
emptied his pockets.

i v .

I think Mother simply gave up.
That she looked at us as something
she once had interest in, like a first-rate
collection of Depression glass or sterling
silver spoons brought back from Mt. Rainier,
Biloxi. I think of that night in the yard,
her floral skirt, light draining away
from the rest of us. How do you see it?
The world is bursting with mysteries.
And you, of course, among them.

v.

Mornings are dark and cool, almost
menacing. The damned minks, for example.
I called Bill and told him to bring his gun.
They've made such a mess of the boat.
Campfires of crayfish claws and shit,
the smell. And then, yesterday, babies.
Not sweet or compelling in any way,
minnows are more endearing. But still,
am I a woman who kills babies?
I phoned Bill back, told him not to come.
There is no telling who I might become.

v i .

Yesterday, cleaning up after them,
I decided to bleach the mildew
from the boat seats. The air was heavy
and I nearly asphyxiated myself.
I had to lie down on the life jackets.
I woke, glasses awry, eyeing my arm
at close range. And then the light
shifted and wind rippled the water's skin,
and the scent of pine and cedar. I was inflated.
I waded into the cold lake in a way I have not
in days, up to my thighs in waves.

vii.

I bet it never crosses your mind, all
the living endure. The constant bird-chirp,
for example, that swoop and prattle.
The promise of mower and chainsaw
revving up the moment you ease
yourself exhausted into the chair,
prop your feet up, breathe. You
take quiet for granted while some days
I'm like a boat lashed in her mooring, bucking
and dropping on the backs of the waves,
or worse, idle when the lake is flat
and dull. But some days I'm just sad.
It's no wonder I fell.

v i i i .

Do you think me greedy? You must.
You who've missed out on this peach-
ripe life. I deny myself next to nothing.
I've quit clipping loosestrife along the shore,
unable to resist its purple stalks. I fold
towels in thirds, stack them in the linen closet,
the warmth off the line. So here I sit, this fine
banana, cold milk, blueberries plump with juice,
and greedy for more. Life is a bruise I keep pressing.
I almost dreamed about you last night but as you
came closer I saw you'd sent your double. What
energy it takes to walk away from your own life.

THREE

Hawaii Volcanoes National Park

February 1992

We arrive late and nearly out of gas,
    weighed down with neither maps
nor common sense. Night comes fast
    here, the short day surprising us.
Walking in flip-flops across a bed
    of Kingsford briquettes, we peer down
into fissures and cracks, edges unstable,
    everything molten glowing below.
We watch lava pour off the rim into
    the Pacific, the ocean's startled hiss.
No one is here to keep us safe.

Fourteen was the last year we really
    had you with us. What I return to
is you eating pineapple for breakfast,
    allowing a lei of orchids in your hair.
In the years since, you've traversed
    your own rifts, shifting ground.
The way Gould begins to play the Goldberg
    variations, then lifts his hands
from the keyboard laughing or talking
    a bit to himself, interrupting what might
have flowed naturally from that point.

THE MOON ISN'T STRONG ENOUGH

The egg shell dropped into the bowl and I understood.
Only a second piece is sharp enough
to lift out what has broken off.

I have raised a child who wanted to kill herself.

One year we hung eggs on a branch of willow.
I was pregnant and queasy. Piercing the shells with a needle,
we blew the insides out. We melted beeswax, drew patterns
on the shells, dipped them in dye baths smelly with vinegar.

The majority never hatch; I dream I am pregnant.

For a year we handled her like Fabergé,
the Resurrection egg, both hemispheres
held together by a belt of rose diamonds.

How gene proud I was, believing I collected her
from the hen house myself one white morning, warmed
her in my cupped hands. Reliable eggs, I thought.
Every 28 days—simple, 12 months, a perfect dozen.

Tonight the moon isn't strong enough to pull an egg,
or it's too bright.

And Sunday night, stacked cages with children inside,
damaged, mostly asleep, except the angry one tethered

to an elastic leash. That one flew at me again and again. I slapped her, shoved her hard. I wanted to see her head crack open, spill its yellow uselessness.

After two days, a chick's heart starts to pump blood.

FORAGE

tries too hard, pokes the snow
for the first sign of spring,
collects wood to stoke her own
fire. She makes no bones about
it; she's always scouring the
ground for something. Her
earliest memory: a repair man
who taught her the right way
to eat a banana: peel, bite, peel,
bite. You want to say, *ease up*,
figure out a way to let some of
it move toward you, pull your
neck in. Forage kills ants in
her cabin if they're not earning
their keep, spares them if they
carry a bread crumb or kernel
of rice. Let them try and creep
across that bare floor with
relaxed, empty jaws and *smack*,
she flattens them.

CHIHULY'S MOUTH

i.

A glass garden in a glass house was how they described
    the exhibit.   I kept thinking, *my girl, my girl,* ringing
        my finger around the rim of this day.

ii.

    Garfield Park Conservatory, thirty installations.
Cobalt reeds sprout beneath a banana palm, forests of glass baskets rest green
                    in dirt, reflect our tired faces.

                        Red stalks and purple spears impale
the sun; orange lily pads the size of hubcaps float in an indoor lake.

iii.

The place you lived that first month
had none of these properties.
    I mean it was the opposite of light.

There was a furnace with a yellow eye, a mattress on the floor
    beside it.   There was you and a casement window
where a muddy world moved past you.

You had one foot in two worlds,
        had drummed with the mad angels who banged
their cups hard on your table, and yet, said you'd smelled
something wild and sweet as the edge of heaven.

        You of all people understood
                glass's split nature.
        Fragile. Tensile.

i v .

        Maybe it's not
like mixing burning seaweed, lime, and sand, holding
        the blowpipe to your lips, kissing
                both reason and lunacy.

        Glass relies on minerals and heat. On chance.
At the intersection of glass and grief, something
        in me smashed to pieces.

v .

In one room, a sea of vessels I returned to over and over,
        relying on their lips, on some opening.

CLOBBER

won't speak to me, he's taken a vow. I
understand he's a construct, not ball pein or
claw; still, he drops like a sledge or stoning
hammer when I don't expect it. Carbon steel,
he resists his neck's natural curve. By twelve
years, his posture was military, vertebrae
clicked into place, secure as rings trapped
on the far side of a swollen knuckle. My
daughter sees his silence differently. She
speaks of the muscles inside the windpipe,
cartilage bands that clench and grip when
you're trying not to cry. *They mirror your
spine*, she tells me. *A kind of pipeline for
voice. They keep your lungs from filling
up with words.*

ESPERANZA

i.

She's coming closer, lets us feed her
green fruit one slice at a time. Esperanza
is greedy for citrus but slow learning
manners. Some nights she gets out
of the cage where we keep her.
We wake to hear pottery dropping
like coconuts onto the hearth.

ii.

I knit her a sweater for cool evenings,
angora with cables, but there is no way
to disguise the truth: She's dangerous, living
in the future as she does, white cyclamen
glowing as she eats its blooms one by one.
Sadness is a locket she wears around
her neck. It is that small.

iii.

She's not like me, leaving a note
for my husband: *starling in the basement,*
then just leaving. A bird in the house

means death. She borrows a net twice
her size, releases the threat into the soft night.
Esperanza thinks of finches exalting
above the creek, that yellow
nothing like the starlings who nested
in our eaves, mobbing other birds.

i v .

After the breakup, they begin fishing
together, swing the battered rowboat on top
of the van with one remaining hubcap.
He casts a perfect arc into Lake Superior,
somehow releasing her father's expensive rod
at the same time. Side by side, they watch
it sink into water too cold to survive in.
He's afraid to face up to his mistake.
Esperanza touches him lightly on the shoulder,
smiles, *You're on your own here.* Rows.

v .

The border collies wear her out, wake
her at two in the morning, demanding
exercise. High-strung, they need their

sheep, their bleats and stampedes. These dogs
don't heel. Their impulse is to gather
the troubled herd, each woolly thought,
heads low while they work.

v i .

One time it was just her and God at the cabin.
God in her All-Stars sipping scotch from a blue cup,
Esperanza hating scotch. God shrugging
when she asked the color of tomorrow's
shoelaces or about the swallows' nest
in the boathouse rafters that summer.
How that mother dive-bombed her, swooped
and feinted to lure her away when she came to swim.
And when it was time for the nestlings to fly, they teetered
on the edge, toppled one by one into the lake and drowned.

A Girl Carries My Blood to California, Claims the Ocean

forty feet from her door brings only dark offerings: waves too cold
and steep to enter, a fading seal, fin ripped off by some rotor, everywhere

the pitch of death. I want to say when you're in the deep, recall the surface.
I want to say here in the midland there's more than tomatoes caged on a deck,

more than gravity's hands at your ankles when you try to fly in your blue
dress. More to life than liver damage, more than the scrawly crow in the yard.

So here is space for grief's fourth rung and bed's soft argument. Not the trees
going green first along the river in spring, not so much potential. I know

you're holy enough to hang icons in an outhouse. I want you scared enough
to carry bug spray and a canary wherever you go, to be a country that padlocks

the doors when death shows up. Earth holds us less securely than the bishop's
weed by the front door, knotted runners extending down where the worms labor

and sigh. Four houses ago, I may have cared more. I know that a blue jay's
wing can imitate a butterfly in leaves and make you think you're seeing

something new. What form of persuasion can I scrounge from these shallow
pockets? Miracles? The fifty bones in your slender feet, the picture

of your grandmother in a pale green gown, the gardenia she wore? Far inland,
I hose down robins, count the *tick tick tick* of the neighbor's sprinkler.

Between dreams I lie awake, anemic moonlight square on the floor, shaped exactly like our window. Still. I want to say that somewhere between grackles

and a white shark there is middle ground: clean sheets on a cool night and a bird that sounds like a swinging gate as you wake. Cabbage moths white as sails.

As surrender flags. I read between your lines: *If it's not broken, it's not mine.*

ORDINARY HOUSE II

Some houses have pygmy goats, grinning like satyrs, beards swishing on their barrel chests, stubby horns pointing. They surround cars that drive up. Not our house. No one here is saving the day. And if it is true that I've begun drinking more and earlier now, if it's true that I wonder about the frogs we find fixed and brittle in the swimming pool we don't use, this is an ordinary house. This is the house which you painted tan, taking months to finish. On the bright side, I painted the door the color of dried blood. Knee deep in spike lavender, I rip binder weed and nightshade from loose chimney bricks. The clusters of dog fur I sweep up become wolf spiders if I let them. Last night nine deer strolled down the street like gunslingers. Where is our shiny red snow blower? Our Lady of the Pretty rain gauge? Comfort shines in the distance, its cold mercury light.

BLANKET

offers comfort. We're all human,
just doing the best we can. She
knows we're afraid, worried
about the snake undulate in the
copper river, the bad apple, that
rattle of paper wasps in the eaves.
Wild turkeys can explode on you,
slashing and pecking as you walk
out to your car. She knows that
a child's face looks monstrous
pressed against a window, lips
splayed flat and gray. She blesses
the woman picked up by a tornado,
then thrown like dice in the path
of a bus. Blanket carries grief in a
satin bag worn under her camisole,
weighted by rocks and other loot
from the pock-faced moon. She
would say we're all just trying to
stay in the saddle, guide our cold
pony home.

THIS SURGERY

was the one where they asked her to stay awake.
They'd show her flash cards, tell her to name

the noun: *car, hammer, grandmother.* As long
as she can say the word, the surgeon continues

to cut out tumor. He didn't worry when suddenly
the house came out *casa*, the shoe, *zapato*. Spanish is,

after all, still language, though not hers. The paring
and then quiet. Words fell away like moths

from snuffed light. No moment when they rattled
like half-dead flies on the attic stairs, no shadows

lengthening into dusk, no bird murmur stilling
before storm. More like a plunge into black water,

the weight of absence pressing against your ears.
The surgeon, reaching the verge of words, stops.

The patient is stunned by pleasure, released
from language, submerged in pure sensation.

No line between light and eyelid, flannel and skin,
that absolute blue arcing from her chest.

OVER AND OVER UNTIL IT STOPS

Already the rough little pony of this new year
    starts to buck and bolt. The holiday's babble
        of gratitude is a town behind us. We know
we've been shot in the eye with luck, still, nothing
    has prepared us to watch our parents empty
        their basement, sort chafing dishes
and manual typewriters, a box of slides carefully
    labeled, "throwaways." It was Anna
who told me, "My children are always trying
        to hurry me from a room." My brothers
    and I don't order a dumpster, we are here to lift
what's too heavy. A squirrel knocks the feeder off its hook,
    spilling thistle seed onto the ground. My father
fills it again, then bumps it, spilling more. When he re-hangs it,
    the squirrel takes two minutes to whack it down.

Setting the table for dinner, I try to remember
    that a match lifted from the wick too soon steals
back its own flame. A woman my age says her parents
    act as though they have 10,000 years to choose
their next home. The family I love is not like that.
    We are greedy as squirrels, know it's all grace:
        the tenderness of husbands, roads black with ice.
            Yellow garbage bags, hair dressers, spatulas. Illnesses
that stop our clock, and bones that won't stop breaking.
    Lemons, teen-aged boys in tuxes playing sax
        and trombone, troubled loves that focus us.

The spill of it, the pony's gallop, the heart's engine cranking
and turning over and over.
O time, your shallow pockets . . . .

LATER I WONDERED IF YOU WERE TALKING ABOUT LIVING

When I dove into the pool all I could do was cry underwater. This was the week you went in the hospital for the first time and I noticed how death watches over his family. I sat on your bed and you told me a story from your childhood. The hired man, how he mowed down the rhubarb thinking it was dock. And how after that, your mother gave up the garden. *We all look for reasons to stop what we don't want to do anymore.*

I Didn't Know I Had Parathyroid glands

until last November when they showed up bad.
The surgeon says "straightforward" *unless*

the glands have migrated to the chest, probably
no overnight stay, probably swimming in a month.

Probably my voice won't be affected. Probably
the anesthesia won't kill me like the two

women my family knew who never came back.
I've always liked my long and scar-free neck,

but I'd also like to sleep more than four hours.
Maybe the nerve trapped in my leg will free itself,

maybe the veins in my legs will disappear, maybe time
will flow backwards and you will not be dead.

You'll be driving me to the pool to spend the afternoon,
wearing sunglasses and that soft white cardigan

loose on your shoulders. And I will be standing
behind you, leaning against the seat.

TODAY DEATH IS THE ANHINGA

we see planted in the wetlands outside
Westlaco, Texas. A woman tells us
to listen for the burping sounds his wings
make when he spreads them out to dry.
Death would burp like that, I think.
Disrespectful. My mother has been dead
nineteen days and this is the kind of detail
I'm looking for. The woman is matter-of-fact
and generous with what she knows. She sells
appliances at Sears and comes to see the birds
on her days off. Thinking about this, I wonder
if I could let the Anhinga simply be the Anhinga,
snake bird, darter. And then, that long neck
undulating above the water line, ready to strike.

Not a House You Can Live in, Cold

as a folding chair in a church basement and nothing plumb.

And now, La La's friend, the psychic, says your dead mother
is not at peace.

You have cried too much, so she's stuck
here in this world collecting your tears in a teacup.

Call this house a scarf where stitches got dropped
in the third row. You can't count on what you know, not

the way hayfeed-to-pasture ratio predicts butterfat in cows.

Or how a car's weight drives frost deeper into the ground.
Not that kind of question. More an economy of cat eyes

at dusk. More like when he drew a line in the dirt out back.
The way your hands ache when you cry. This house

has stink bugs and broken snakes, gas leaks, inbred stars
tommy-gunned into the night like Jimmy's Zippo collection.

You miss your mother enough to smell her in the night. She's the one
who slept in front of the door to keep it shut. She taught you

if potato slices on the forehead don't drain fever, cross
the body with raw eggs till the whites cook.

Whatever Shines

Already the jeweler has come to love me. He loves
your ring. He inspects the mountings, coaches me
on how to pamper it. It should have its own soft
pouch to rest in, never leave it on the lip of the sink.
Diamonds love their friends. Joy and ammonia make
them flash. I'm learning the nature of unwanted
gifts.

He reminds me that this ring already has forty
years of wear. I was living above a river in France
the month you got it. He calls his colleagues to look,
invites me to view it under his microscope. Every
facet throws light.

When I told you I might change the setting, you
gave permission but said, *It won't be as pretty.* I'm
getting used to it. Every day it grows smaller on my
hand.

THE NEXT-TO-LAST THING
MY MOTHER TAUGHT ME

was how to put in her hearing aids, flesh
colored shells tucked into each canal,
right ear coded red, left marked blue.

At night, lift the little switch to conserve
the battery. Hold it close to your ear to test
its power and see if it whistles.

You had stopped caring about your glasses
but every morning before I brought
your orange juice, this ritual. I felt

like a good girl. Then one day you pushed
my hand away. After you died, and I stepped
into Dad's arms, his hearing aid wailed.

THE THERAPIST CONSIDERS THE EVIDENCE

My eyes rise from the line on the window
where the Windex gave out, and there

it is, nest the size of a bear cub wedged
into the crook of this junk tree. Mirage

of stability, constructed entirely of leaves
and smudge, one shudder from plunge.

This pain accumulates, bird with its head
stapled under its wing, boy on a hook

in the barn, bat caught in a dental floss noose.
Cameras like mirrors and clocks like hearts.

Waiting for a new tremor in his daughter's hand,
or the blue butterfly they mounted on a piece

of slate after her funeral. The moment when
her husband won't look her in the eye.

The seven-second tour they called it
at the Grand Canyon, where one step back

to frame a mule's face in the lens finder,
and swoosh! One minute we're admiring

the catalpa leaves, hearty as pie plates, the next,
this dirty den fifty feet in the air, full of pill vials

and broken teeth, crutches and puppets and feathers
and lice, hurtling straight at the window.

How I Feel When It Stops

It started when my husband left,
a steady sluice of water without
wind. No deluge, just constancy.
I sort paper, the slowest purge, each
printed sheet requiring deliberation,

progress imperceptible. I wear a blue
slicker to walk the dog and note
sidewalks afloat in places, sewers
that gush and prosper. By the second
day, it is beginning to feel biblical.

I think of my husband up north
with his only friend and how much I love
an empty house, but only because
I believe he is coming home,
the way I believe the rain will stop.

There is no narrative arc here. The rain
is the story. Sunday: the grocery
store, the slicker, the dog, the rain, water
climbing steps, or slipping one long leg
through the basement window. A man

and his son kayak on Crosstown
Parkway. The duck ponds have left
their banks and headed south. White

mushrooms the size of toasters spring
up on my neighbor's lawn and our own

basement wall is seeping. I sleep better
than I have in years, dream about
wading boots which as a child I thought
were waiting boots, because I was always
waiting for my grandfather who wore them.

I've been waiting for a sign
from the world at large. I want
word from something small
and reliable—snake, frog, butterfly—
anything that transforms itself.

When it finally stops, I'll be in the dark
watching a movie where each scene
includes wine, noticing how *wine* and *rain*
sound nearly alike. Waiting for some
unknotting, resignation or acceptance.

If Marriage Is a Constellation

How many stars and how dark must it get
for them to shine? We live on the wrong

side of Lake Michigan, its cold breath
condensing in this state the shape

of a sassafras leaf. Richard
took a stargazing class and six

Thursdays in a row found each
expected pattern buried by clouds.

And if marriage is a mason jar, how
many butterflies can it hold, their wings,

blue or pale yellow made of dust, easily
crushed by your thumb, my blunt tongue?

What are we to make of the gold ring
that screws the thing together? It's hard

to find a map to marriage, glove box full
of receipts, flashlight with dead batteries.

Maybe I'll find the map in the river, see
marks you made in the margin, reminder

to keep casting our net toward shadow.
I remember that first April, watching

men dip smelt, how the water ran fast
and black with bodies.

PILFER

is disappointed when she wakes
from a dream, learns she's not in
Greece, that she doesn't own the
ring that she'd stolen there. She
wants to have thin legs, a neck
arched as an arpeggio. She suffers
object lust: green bowls with
cream interiors, a hummingbird
nest. She hoards what doesn't
belong to her, sees a jet stream and
wants two, believes she deserves
the moon and its ransom note,
the snow turning blue in the late
afternoon, voices sounding across
the field as if over water. She
wants the ice beads on the sumac
bush, the feathers on the cardinal.
Pilfer resents a day without deer
and then when she sees them she
wants what they have: black lips,
beds in the snow, each other.

GLOCK

It suits me, not quite as reliable
as a revolver but more elegant.
Small and light, hardly any recoil.
Actually, I love it. Dick is the first
to drop. I didn't see it happen but
I'm sure he's the one who backed
into my front fender, unhinging it
slightly.

If Marriage Is a Rowboat Full of Bees

This boat's not aluminum, the kind that flashes sun,
easy to strap on the car roof for a fishing trip out of town.

This boat is long-leaf yellow pine, not rotted, but sodden,
taking in waves that clench and sidle around it. It floats low.

If we lived in an ordinary house, the answer might be
a husband bringing home another dozen eggs. A woman ironing

in front of a window. But out here? Some bailing and wringing,
some sucking it up, a big sand-colored sponge. No one believes

this boat can be sunk by bees, the weight of fiery bodies,
deaf and accustomed to the dark hive, bees who rely on touch,

on figure-8 dances, now push and pull under a night sky
in a rocking boat. It's not our fault. We don't notice

till after we lower ourselves into its buzzing belly, this hull
full of sweet-seekers. A rowboat, risk extending in all directions.

ORDINARY HOUSE III

Not a rock and a hard place this time, more
like the spot between divorce and deciding
to remodel the kitchen. A daughter says
if we were strung any tighter we'd be harps.
It takes three rice sacks, heated, to replace
a husband in bed and we're midway
between hooking the gate and lickety-split.
The fuse box and running shoes. Somewhere
between slurping soup and uprooting the tree,
insight could be looming. Don't bet the rent.
How many can swerve to dodge a deer in the road
and not overcorrect? We ease lightness back
and forth between us, abacus beads on wire.

WHY THE THERAPIST LOVES IRONING

Sometimes my urge to iron surges beyond trousers
and hankies. My daughter says it's a colonial impulse,

*a progressive narrative, Mom, a linear press toward
improvement.* I disagree with that architect in Vienna

who designed and built only organic shapes, believing
evil followed straight lines. My mother stepped

on a tarantula in Honduras, moments after eating two
bananas so perfect she swore she'd never eat another.

The promises we fail to keep. Did I promise not to kill
spiders? Suddenly, it's not enough to flatten gingko leaves,

sassafras, catalpas bigger than the pages of my heaviest book.
The pin cherry, its orderly thoughts, its fruit named for hat pins,

makes me want to squash spiders in the family Bible, sandwich
them in wax paper. Maybe a flower press, turning the screws

gradually. Some days I want to press fingertips over my mouth,
hands over my ears. What could it hurt, red leaves flattened

on the lapels of the bereaved? Hope fixed with a sadiron onto despair?
I sit with a soldier who says in Iraq they have camel spiders huge

as her stepfather's hand. Ironing's the opposite of grave rubbing.
My mother told me she prayed each day she'd die before my father.

How It Begins

I take a long walk and find myself thinking *hey, this dog doesn't have a mood disorder.* Or I hear my husband in the kitchen below and wonder how he makes so much noise with dishes and water. From this window, two nuthatches flirt with gravity, sweet-gum leaves spread out like stars on the lawn. I remember deer kissing each other on their black lips outside our cabin. Mark said they were grooming each other for lice. But I was witness and I could tell it was something more. And the third one, awkward, looking on.

Acknowledgments

I am grateful to the following journals in which these poems first appeared, some in slightly different form or under different titles.

Alaskan Quarterly Review: "Sometimes Night Is a Creek Too Wide to Leap"

Bellevue Literary Review: "Why the Therapist Loves Ironing"

Indiana Review: "How I Feel When It Stops"

Poet-Lore: "Not a House You Can Live in, Cold"; "The Next-to-Last Thing My Mother Taught Me"

Poetry East: "I Don't Want to Say How Lost I've Been"; "Uncoupling"

Prairie Schooner: "Esperanza"; "This Surgery"

Primavera: "When Pippi Longstocking Was My Mother"

Rattle: "Juggler"

The Southern Review: "Augenblick"

Tar River Poetry: "Over and Over Until It Stops"; "The Therapist Watches Birds"

Third Coast: "The Moon Isn't Strong Enough"

West Branch: "Ordinary House II" (as "Some Houses Have Pygmy Goats")

"I Don't Want to Say How Lost I've Been" was reprinted in *Poetry in Michigan/ Michigan in Poetry*, edited by William Olsen and Jack Ridl, published by New Issues, 2013

Deep gratitude and love to Conrad Hilberry, Christine Horton, Kit Almy, Danna Ephland, Susan Ramsey, Marie Bahlke, and Marion Boyer who have helped make these poems—and Sunday afternoons—so much better!

Thank you to Diane Seuss, Traci Brimhall, Susan Ramsey, Patrick Donnelly, and Kathleen McGookey, who read earlier versions of the book, raising good questions and answering others. Thank you also to Laura Kasischke and Bonnie Jo Campbell for your votes of confidence.

Thanks to all the Dawgs, past and present, coming and going, for friendship, good humor, and high standards.

To Pam Poley who has offered in generous measure, her presence, love, wisdom, and support for many years. I have leaned on it.

To my beloveds, Sarah, Bailey, and Katy, whose love is tucked in my pocket and who always have my back—in ways both fierce and tender.

I am grateful to the Glen Arbor Art Association for offering me a residency to work in such a beautiful part of our state during the early stages of this book.

Thank you to Susan Kan for choosing to publish my book, and then nudging me to look at ways to make it better.

About the Author

Gail Martin's first book is *The Hourglass Heart* (New Issues Press, 2003). She is a Michigan native with deep roots in both southern and northern Michigan. She works as a psychotherapist in private practice in Kalamazoo, where she lives with her husband, George, and her dog, Piper.

ABOUT PERUGIA PRESS

Perugia Press publishes one collection of poetry each year, by a woman at the beginning of her publishing career. Our mission is to produce beautiful books that interest long-time readers of poetry and welcome those new to poetry. We also aim to celebrate and promote poetry whenever we can, and to keep the cultural discussion of poetry inclusive.

Also from Perugia Press:
- *The Wishing Tomb*, Amanda Auchter
- *Gloss*, Ida Stewart
- *Each Crumbling House*, Melody S. Gee
- *How to Live on Bread and Music*, Jennifer K. Sweeney
- *Two Minutes of Light*, Nancy K. Pearson
- *Beg No Pardon*, Lynne Thompson
- *Lamb*, Frannie Lindsay
- *The Disappearing Letters*, Carol Edelstein
- *Kettle Bottom*, Diane Gilliam Fisher
- *Seamless*, Linda Tomol Pennisi
- *Red*, Melanie Braverman
- *A Wound On Stone*, Faye George
- *The Work of Hands*, Catherine Anderson
- *Reach*, Janet E. Aalfs
- *Impulse to Fly*, Almitra David
- *Finding the Bear*, Gail Thomas

This book was typeset in Aldus, a type family designed in 1954 by German type designer Hermann Zapf, as a text face to complement Palatino, with which it shares many design characteristics. It is both more delicate than Palatino and also engineered to reproduce more legibly when printed in small sizes.